The End Times
within God's Overall Biblical Plan and Purpose for Mankind

Henry A. Field

Copyright © December 2020 Henry A. Field

All rights reserved. No part of this book may be reproduced in any form or by any electronic or mechanical means, including information storage and retrieval systems, without permission in writing from the publisher, except by reviewers, who may quote brief passages in a review.

First Printing: December 2020
Printed by IngramSpark
ISBN: 978-1-8382976-0-2

Almighty God has a special, awesome Plan and Purpose for Mankind in Man's history on this Earth, and beyond, which is too good to miss!!!

The plan is God's overall strategy and I will give it below, in diagram form, to simplify it and give the reader a bird's eye view of what it is. God's purpose is very simple – it is to obtain a number, which only Father God knows, from all of Mankind who have ever lived on this Earth, who will, out of their freedom of choice, thought and action, give themselves to Him. This will not be by coercion or any kind of control {robotic, computer chip or any other form} – not as conscripts but volunteers – and not of their minds and wills only but they, by belief, trust and humility, will fall in love with God because of His love to them. They will, in spite of sin and the working of God's enemies, give Him their hearts and lives, so as to have Him live with them in their hearts. This will be not only for their time on Earth but for life's other side in what God has for them, living with Him and with those in Heaven, forever. He will make the only way for the above through His Son, the Saviour {the Lord Jesus...Messiah...the Anointed One from Heaven}. God will test, fairly and kindly, all those who get right with Him to prove that they are fit to live with Him now and in Heaven forever.

The Trinity

God is One yet the Godhead is Three in One – a perfect Unity and Family – Three in One and One in Three – as someone said, 'One in essence but Three in personality' – all equal but with different roles – Father, Son and Holy Spirit. The role of Father God is 'Managing Director/CEO'. He is in overall control, everything is under Him, there is nothing and no-one above Him. He is all-knowing, all-powerful, just/fair in all that He does, good, righteous etc. Love, holiness, glory, majesty and much more are all His. God the Father gives the orders in and from Heaven and they are obeyed and fulfilled.

The Son is 'the Manager', the begotten Son of God, the Saviour {Jesus} Messiah {the Anointed One} from Heaven and is now King of Heaven and Earth - that is of all those on Earth who have truly given their hearts to Him. The Lord Jesus (Christ), being fully man and fully God, was tested, on Earth, for thirty-three and a half years and never once sinned so was able to give His life as a perfect sacrifice on Calvary's cruel Cross to die for the sins of Mankind and thus to redeem {buy back} those who choose to give Him their heart and so to reconcile them to Father God.

The Holy Spirit is 'the Worker/Creator' who does the Father's bidding to go forth and work as He directs. Heaven is made up of all angelic beings who did not rebel and follow Satan, the devil, also all human beings since Adam and Eve who got right with God.

The Warfare we are in

Behind the physical is the spiritual – the spiritual, which will last forever, is more important than the physical. The problem is there is a mighty war and battle going on between the forces of good that are of God, which includes those, in truth, who are **with** and **for** Him i.e. on **His** side....and....on the other side, against God, are all those who, by default or otherwise, belong to the forces of darkness and evil under the devil, Satan/Lucifer, the fallen angel from Heaven who served God then rebelled, taking many other angels with him in his anarchy then also taking fallen, sinful Mankind onto his side by deception, destruction, violence, corruption etc. He set out to destroy God's rule in Heaven and then on Earth. Later he fought against the Son of God, Jesus the Messiah, by severely testing Him by trying to tempt Him to sin but just before, and at, Calvary's Cross, Satan totally lost all by Messiah's love, action, sacrifice of Himself and finished work on Calvary's Cross. He, Jesus, as the Spotless Lamb of God, was crucified but Mankind could not take His life from Him and that is why He said, 'It is finished' as He had done all He came to Earth to do and then gave up His spirit to Father God and His soul and spirit departed from His body – His flesh became dead at that point. This took place at the Jewish Festival of Passover, then on the third day after that, Jesus was resurrected from the dead so that He could/would take all those who believe in Him and give them the free gift of Eternal Life to have Him in their heart and so to be with Him forever.

The war has been won by the Lord Jesus at Calvary {just outside Jerusalem} but the battles still rage as Father God's plan is being accomplished. Certain things still have to happen but we, as Mankind, are now near the end of the present 'Age of Grace' and Father God is about to move things on to the next stage of His plan. When we grasp all of this it gives us a different perspective on life, wisdom and understanding from above. The whole book of Revelation, in the Bible, is important, and within the Book of Daniel {also in the Bible} there is given a superb insight into the warfare we are currently in and how it works for and against us.

Time

God is infinite and in eternity. Nothing is impossible with God and, within the rules He made, He will do whatever He pleases. There is no 'time' in Heaven – God is outside of 'time' in eternity, in fact He had to miraculously create 'time' in our world for our benefit. There are no clocks and, as I understand it, there is no beat in Heaven. Heavenly music/worship can stop and start and is a continuous sound without a beat. There is also melody in Heaven. The celestial bodies around the Earth – sun, moon and planets are all involved with our 'time'. Their movements, past present and future, can be worked out exactly because of God's amazing synchronization in creation.

Numbers

Numbers and words are important to God and numbers, in the Bible, do have meaning eg 5 is linked to grace {undeserved favour}, 4 refers to the Earth, the number 7, with some of its multiples, is very important to Father God. The number 7 in the Bible means spiritual perfection. 1000 years, from God's perspective, is just like one day and one day, to Him, is just like 1000 years. *{See 2 Peter chapter 3 verse 8* and *Psalm 90 verse 4* in the Bible}. 'The Millennium' {see diagram below} is 1000 years in Man's time and is as one day to God. The words 'dispensation' and 'age' are found in *Ephesians chapter 3 verses 1 to 5* and both words are used to show that God is dealing with one or more lengthy periods of time {see in diagram below}. For the purpose of this book I am using the words 'dispensation' and 'age' as interchangeable.

Mankind

Mankind is made in the image of God, which I understand to be – body, soul {mind, emotion, will}, spirit and conscience – distinct from all animals and anything else in creation. *Psalm 139* shows that we are 'fearfully and wonderfully made' by God. We are complex beings, privileged and very special to God, but sin, of course, has marred this relationship. {We are all born as sinners, coming down the line from Adam and Eve who chose to sin, and so broke Mankind's perfect relationship with God.}

Controversial Issues………. Jews and Israel

God made the Jews, and Israel as a country, to be very gifted and to be special, with the purpose of being a lead nation on this Earth. I believe this will fully happen during 'The Millennium'. To the Jews was given the Messiah from Heaven!

Heaven and Hell

The Bible tells us very clearly that the Lord Jesus talked about and believed in the reality of Heaven and of Hell {e.g. see *Luke chapter 16, Matthew chapter 25, Mark chapter 9*} - surely this is a warning for us to choose Heaven and, at any cost, avoid Hell! What you decide down here on Earth, before you eventually go to life's other side, will show where, by your own choice, you will spend eternity *{John chapter 3 verse 16}*. At any cost, make sure you get born again by giving your heart to the Lord Jesus and, if you mean it, your sins will be forgiven and your name will be written in Jesus, the Lamb of God's Book of Life. Do not get yourself too far away from God …. beyond forgiveness! *{See Psalm 73 verses 25 – 28, especially verse 27.}*

The Holy Spirit Baptism

God gives us His Holy Spirit to be 'with us' on Earth to convict us of our sins/wrongs. When we get born again {born spiritually by giving Him our heart} the Holy Spirit comes 'into' our heart to show us we belong to Him. There is also another experience, available to us, called the 'Baptism of the Holy Spirit' which comes 'upon us' to flood us with His love and much more. This happened to me over 40 years ago in an awesome way, but a long time after that I was accused of being evil because different people in the Church wouldn't accept it had been a God-given experience, although *Acts chapters 1 and 2*, for example, show clearly that it is!

As I stated earlier, God is Love and is just and fair. His love made the way for us to be brought from our sinful state into a love relationship with Him – all through the shedding of the Blood of His Son, the Lord Jesus, the perfect sacrifice, just before, and at, Calvary's horrifically cruel Cross. Such love is incredible!

Important information relating to the diagrams below

As I understand it, the 7 days or 7000 years of Mankind on Earth, as shown below in the first diagram, consist of 3 x 2000 years and 1 x 1000 years. The 3 x 2000 years are: 'Conscience'; 'The Law'; 'The Dispensation of God's Grace and Mercy'. The last of these three is where we, as Mankind, are now and it is coming to an end shortly. To get from now {December 2020} into God's 'Millennium Rest Day' for Mankind on Earth there must be a major sorting out by the Trinity of God and the angelic host of Heaven to get the various peoples of the Earth exactly where God wants them to be, and this will include nations/people who will go into the Age of the Millennium and populate the Earth, and most of them, I would say, will see, in their very old age, the end of The Millennium. {God always has His 'Rest Day' and wants us to have ours, so we are supposed to always have one day off out of seven, as needful for Mankind. In the 1950s our Sunday off was generally a day of rest and a 'family day' to practise and remember our Christian heritage.}

The news for the people on Earth currently worried about the likes of climate change etc. is that for, and in, The Millennium, God the Father will sort it all out, all the time, for both humanity and the animals so that it will be perfect and peaceful for all of the Earth – no concern about weather, climate change, food or anything else! It might seem strange to say but there is no record of anyone becoming a believer during The Millennium. In the Bible, the Prophet Isaiah gives us some clear glimpses of this time.

Just before the time of The Millennium there will be almost 7 years of tribulation {trouble} on the whole Earth. See diagrams. In 'The Tribulation' there will be untold suffering, through total control by the forces of evil, yet all those who refuse to accept 'the chip' {see below} and want to give their hearts to the Lord Jesus Christ will be able to do so although it may well mean real suffering.

Several important things must happen just before, and at, the actual time of the start of The Tribulation. *(1 Thessalonians chapter 4 verse 17)* The true 'Church' worldwide, i.e. all born again believers who are still alive on Earth, will be removed from the Earth to above the clouds to meet, in the air, the Lord Jesus, along with all those He brings with Him from Heaven {who had been born again when alive on Earth earlier in this 'Age of Grace'.... 'Days 5 and 6' – see diagram below}.... and all go off to Heaven to the wedding of the Bride {i.e. all believers} to the Bridegroom {i.e. the Lord Jesus}. God's spotlight, as it were, will now go onto the Jews, Israel and, in particular, Jerusalem. The 'Antichrist' will appear as 'another Christ' and will fool all the nations into thinking **he** is the 'Messiah Jesus' and many will be deceived. My understanding is that he will control the peoples of the Earth by a computer chip or something similar, with its 666 whatever, implanted in their right hand or forehead and that only those who accept 'the chip' {or similar} will be able to buy or sell, and that this controlling will be done via the internet, in a cashless society, with a view to controlling the whole world {which he will not achieve}. I believe each 6 (of 666) will actually be a series of 6 numbers, so, in total, 18 numbers and that, by computer electronics, every person in the world will be numbered. Those who do accept 'the chip' {or similar} will never be able to get right with the Trinity of God {i.e. unable to be born again} so must go later to the fires of Hell {*Revelation chapter 14 verses 9 – 11*}.

At the end of The Tribulation, when Messiah Jesus returns to Earth, He will sort out the 'sheep' and 'goat' nations, getting rid of the latter and ushering the former i.e. the 'sheep nations', with Israel leading, into the 1000 years of The Millennium to populate the Earth for God's Millennium 'Rest Day'. This is the moment that Messiah Jesus will start His 1000 year reign from the new Temple built in Jerusalem (I would say at the beginning of The Tribulation period).

My third diagram below indicates briefly what will take place at that time, and on into Eternity.

Part of the Book of Revelation, the last Book in the Bible, gives a lot of information as to what will happen in The Tribulation, and the Book of Daniel, the Prophet, also gives some interesting information regarding the Jews and Israel at the time of The Tribulation e.g. that the second half of The Tribulation will be worse than the first half, and that half way through The Tribulation all the Jews in Israel will fully believe that Jesus is their promised Messiah. Because the Jews are appointed by God as The Lead Nation of the World they will suffer persecution during The Tribulation but during the latter half of The Tribulation they will have a special, supernatural protection from God in His Heaven. The Tribulation will be the worst time ever on Earth and will be like the Roman Empire returning – the Romans and their armies were horrifically cruel.

To you, as the reader, - I beg you to give your heart to the Lord Jesus now and be born again, born spiritually, to make sure you will go to Heaven and avoid going through The Tribulation! As we know, 'chips' are currently being implanted in dogs and other animals – please do not ever agree to having one implanted in your body – Satan and the forces of evil are not allowed to give you 'the chip' unless you agree to accept it – please do not ignore this warning!

Diagrams, Headings and Notes

As stated above, God is outside of 'Time' and in 'Eternity'.

As *Psalm 90 verse 4* explains, 1000 of Mankind's Earth years are as one day to God in His Heaven. Man's history is 7 days in total and therefore 7000 years. It is divided into three sections of 'Ages' of 2000 years each and one section of 1000 years.

The subjects covered in the three actual diagrams may also be covered in the main body of written work in this book as repeat or further information.

Diagram 1

The Age of the first 2 days	The Age of the second 2 days	(3) THE MESSIAH ON EARTH & CALVARY'S CROSS	The Age of the third 2 days	THE TRIBULATION	The Age of the Seventh day	GOD'S FINAL JUDGEMENT	
(1) AGE OF CONSCIENCE AND GIVING THANKS TO GOD (Romans 1 v 21)	(2) AGE OF THE LAW AND ORDER		(4) AGE OF GRACE AND MERCY	[b]	AGE OF THE MILLENNIUM [c]	[d]	THE ETERNAL STATE
Two days or 2 x 1000 years	Two days or 2 x 1000 years	[a]	Two days or 2 x 1000 years		The final one day on Earth of 1000 years		

[a] see section (3) …. The ultimate sacrifice of the Lord Jesus at Calvary's Cross

[b] see diagram 2, what happens just before and the time of the 7 of man's years of tribulation

[c] see below for what takes place at these times, see diagram 3

[d] known as The Great White Throne Judgement

Please note - Diagrams 2 and 3 enlarge on information given in Diagram 1

1. The Age of Conscience

This Age can be called the 'Age of Conscience' {see Genesis, the first Book of the Bible} because during the first 2000 years the way to God for Mankind was via one's 'conscience' by a knowing from, and a pleasing of, God, in one's choice of right over wrong, good over bad, by obeying the 'knowledge from God implanted within our being'. {It is worth repeating that no other creature in God's creation has a conscience.} Only Noah and his wife and family all obeyed their God-given conscience and followed His instructions – these eight people were saved by their obedience while every other human being on Earth perished in The Flood. See *Romans chapter 1 verses 19-21, especially verse 21*, which I believe is also applicable – choose right not wrong i.e. follow your conscience, and it's also important to give God the thanks, praise and worship due to Him for who He is and for His beautiful creation, in spite of Mankind's sins.

2. The Age of The Law

This Age can be called the 'Age of The Law' because during the second 2000 years the way to God was via keeping His special Law called The Mosaic Law i.e. The Law given supernaturally by God to Moses who was in charge of the Hebrews, later called the Jews, in the Land of Israel.

Law is a system of rules and regulations of a country or community, with binding forces and penalties if not obeyed. The first five books of the Bible, called The Torah by the Jews, and called The Pentateuch by Christians, is the part of the Bible where we find the detailed Law of God. Leviticus {3rd Book of The Pentateuch} gives a massive amount of detail {mirrored somewhat in Deuteronomy, 5th Book of The Pentateuch} on the do's and don'ts, rules and regs, all the animal sacrifices, the reason for them and administration of them, the fasts and feasts that had to be kept plus observation of sacred days and festivals etc. These laws, as appropriate, applied to individuals through to the whole nation – there were penalties for disobedience, with the religious leaders in charge being, as it were, the 'police force' and the high up political class.

With regard to the animal sacrificial system – the penalty of sin is death and because 'the life is in the blood' the bloodshed and death of the animal, instead of the death of the person/people who had sinned, was accepted by God the Father so the death of the animal involved, in the way directed by God, if correctly administered, brought forgiveness and let the person/people come back into a right relationship with God. This was a repetitive ongoing system and it all pointed to what the Messiah was going to do in the Age of Grace.

Two abbreviated summaries of The Law found in the Bible are The Ten Commandments in *Exodus chapter 20* and then in *Matthew chapter 22 verses 36-39* where Jesus said in response to the question,

'Which is the greatest commandment in The Law?'

"Love the Lord your God with all your heart, all your soul and all your mind....and the second is like it, love your neighbour as yourself."

Three relevant references to The Law out of several given in the New Testament are:

1a. *Galatians chapter 3 verses 23-25* where The Law is likened to a schoolmaster guiding the way towards the Lord Jesus.... 'Before the way of faith in Christ was available to us, we were placed under guard by The Law. We were kept in protective custody, so to speak, until the way of faith was revealed. Let me put it another way. The Law was our guardian {schoolmaster} until Christ came, it protected us until we could be made right with God through faith. {And now that the way of faith has come, we no longer need The Law as our guardian.}'

1b. *John chapter 1 verse 17*

'For The Law was given through Moses, but grace and truth came through Jesus Christ.' We are freed from The Law through what Jesus did – see below in the 'Age of Grace'.

1c. *Galatians chapter 5 verse 18*

'If you are led by the Spirit of God you are not under The Law' {so you are free from The Law and all its legalism}.

3. The Ultimate Sacrifice of The Lord Jesus at Calvary's Cross

I have already covered some of what follows below under 'The Plan and Purpose of God for Mankind' and what the Lord Jesus did.

"It's a new covenant {vow/agreement} in My Blood" said the Lord Jesus – The Age of The Law was coming to an end! After exactly thirty-three and a half years of life on this Earth, when the Lord Jesus said on Calvary's Cross, "It is finished!" that, I would say, was the exact moment of the end of the 'Age of The Law' {although some might say that Pentecost [*Acts chapters 1 and 2*] was the moment}. Those thirty-three and a half years of the Lord's life on Earth, with all His trials and testings and all that was fulfilled by Jesus, fitted miraculously exactly into the end of the 'Age of The Law' and led straight into the 'Age of Grace and Mercy'. This meant it was ALL CHANGE!

Mankind could not keep The Law of God so had to keep on repeating the animal sacrifices as a cover for sin, but the new covenant in the Blood of Jesus at Calvary's Cross, was a once for all, never to be repeated, sacrifice of Himself by the Lord Jesus, the shedding of His Blood as a cover for sin – an incredible free gift on offer to Mankind! Everything about this new covenant between the Trinity of God and sinful Mankind was done on God's side – we, as Mankind, could not do anything to bring it about – there are certain conditions afterwards which we need to abide by but it's great news that Mankind definitely had no part in making the covenant which means we couldn't mess it up/break it. It was given out in mercy, grace and love to us as a free gift.

The Lord Jesus, by His perfect, sinless life, fulfilled all the requirements/conditions of The Law for Mankind so that all Mankind has to do is to believe in Him, give the Lord Jesus his/her heart, in love and humility, in response to Father God's great love, and so come into a full relationship with Him that will last forever and never be undone. The Law of itself could not do this but the Lord Jesus, during His thirty-three and a half years on this Earth, kept The Law in full, so if we believe and give Him our heart, then, with us in Him, and Him in us, we are totally free from The Law. When we show in faith, hope and trust, that we do believe and want to accept God's amazing free, beautiful gift of His grace, mercy and love, by His Holy Spirit coming into our heart, then a wonderful 'Divine Exchange' takes place.

In this Divine Exchange God takes all that is bad about us {Jesus took the punishment, due to us for our sins, on Calvary's Cross} and He gives us everything good about Him – this is all done by Him, on His side, in response to our belief and acceptance of His free gift of forgiveness. Yes, as believers, we should take bread and wine now and again as symbolic remembrance of what the enormous cost of His death on the Cross was for Him, and we should be baptised in water {by total immersion if possible} to represent His life, death and resurrection from the dead to give us life in Heaven forever.

4. The Age of Grace and Mercy

This Age can be called the {fabulous} 'Age of Grace {undeserved/unmerited favour} and God's Mercy and Love' because during the third 2000 years which we, in 2020, are currently living in, the way to God, as I have already explained above, is via His amazingly merciful offer of 'Divine Exchange' as a free gift to those who choose, by faith, to accept it. This Age of Grace and Mercy is nearing its end and God is about to move things on to the next stage of His plan.

We live in an incredible time as God 'sets the stage', as it were, for what lies just ahead i.e. The Tribulation {see below}. Everything that is happening, all the computer, internet, electronic stuff etc. is part of the 'setting of the stage' and God's anger is against our sinful world which mostly does not want Him, in spite of all that the Lord Jesus went through for us to have a powerful relationship with Him and Father God, and the awesome 'package' gifted to those who believe.

In addition to what I've already explained above about the 'Divine Exchange' let me select for you some headings/comments regarding the truly wonderful {in reality it's 'the tops'!} 'package' of what God has done/is doing for us in this soon-to-end Age of Grace and Mercy i.e. for those of us who choose to believe all that Jesus has done for us and who take this 'package' by believing and acting on His Word.

My not – exhaustive list of headings/comments

These are not in any particular order but show just some of what the Trinity of God gives, in this 'package', to us who believe on Him here on Earth … WOW!!!

Forgiveness

When Father God, through the finished work of the Lord Jesus at Calvary's Cross, forgives us for our sins against Him, Heaven, others and ourselves, we must, by our heart and will, forgive those who have sinned against/wronged us and leave it all with God. It can be a time of real healing eg *Luke chapter 15 verse 21* – the Prodigal Son.

Freedom

When we understand and walk in the freedom that Christ Jesus gives us it is truly amazing! We are free from the bondage of The Law, and the closer we get to God, from the tyranny of sin.

Galatians chapter 5 verse 1

'Stand fast therefore in the liberty by which Christ has made us free….'

John chapter 8 verse 36

'If the Son makes you free you shall be free indeed.'

Romans chapter 8 verse 2

'Jesus has made me free from the law of sin and death.'

John chapter 8 verse 32

'The truth will set you free.'

The Priesthood

Jesus is our great 'High Priest' and, as His sons and daughters, we, as truly born-again believers, are **all** priests. A priest represents others and himself/herself to Father God with 24/7 access to Father God and, if done in righteousness, he/she will have God's 'ear' in presenting petitions/requests to Him. 'Priesthood' is not just for a few people chosen by others to be 'Priests' but for every one of us who is a born-again believer!

1 Peter chapter 2 verses 5,9

Revelation chapter 1 verse 6

The Holy Spirit

Acts chapters 1, 2

God, the Holy Spirit, is 'with us' to convict us of sin then, if we become believers, He comes, at that very moment, to dwell 'in us', in our hearts – also He comes powerfully 'upon us' at the 'Baptism of the Holy Spirit' and may continue to anoint us/empower us to accomplish what God wants us to do, or to be, when we ask Him to do so, and when Father God chooses or wills for it to happen to us.

The Fruit of The Holy Spirit

Galatians chapter 5 verses 22 and 23

When we become believers the Holy Spirit comes into our heart and His work is to produce 'fruit' in our lives. This 'fruit' is "love, joy, peace, patience, kindness, goodness, faithfulness, gentleness, self-control. Against such there is no law."

His work in us continues throughout the remainder of our lives, transforming us to live as God desires. These nine attributes 'love, joy, peace, patience, kindness, goodness, faithfulness, gentleness, self-control' should increase in measure in our lives when we choose to live, in accord with the Holy Spirit, in a way that pleases God, by us allowing the Holy Spirit to produce this kind of 'fruit' {love, joy....self-control} in our lives despite the fact that we still sin.

These nine attributes show the lovely character of God, in full measure always, and cannot be separated from Him. He also has many other wonderful characteristics e.g. justice and wisdom….and He is infinite!

Freedom, and Gifts from the Trinity of God to His Church in the Age of Grace

Currently in the UK we generally have the freedom to be who we are and to make choices e.g. where to live/work, which belief system or organization we choose to belong to. The spiritual freedom around us, given by God, is real freedom. Evil spiritual forces around us anywhere, e.g. dictatorship, will destroy our freedom and put us into bondage.

Every born-again believer has at least one God-given gift. This gift is given to help to make the Church mature, healthy, strong and powerful so as to take on the forces of evil, sin, wickedness, deception and lies from the pit of Hell.

See *Romans chapter 12 verses 6-8* re seven gifts given by God the Father {prophesying, serving, teaching, exhortation [encouragement], giving, leadership, mercy}. See *1 Corinthians chapter 12 verses 4-11* and *1 Corinthians chapter 14* re nine gifts given by the Holy spirit {words of wisdom, words of knowledge, faith, healing, miracles, prophecy, distinguishing between spirits, speaking in tongues [languages], interpretation of tongues}. See E*phesians chapter 4 verse 11*, in its context, re five gifts of 'offices', {I say, as in full-time work} given by the Lord Jesus, which carry a great deal of responsibility and are for the mature in Christ, prepared over a period of time {apostles, prophets, evangelists, pastors, teachers}. Also see *1 Corinthians chapter 12 verse 28* for a helpful list given by God {apostles, prophets, teachers – given in that order of importance, then miracles, healings, helps [caring/helping other people], administrations, varieties of tongues}.

As a young believer, in the early 1970s, I was greatly influenced by {the now late} Selwyn Hughes, a powerful man of God with a writing ministry. He was also a pastor-teacher and evangelist and gave excellent teaching on the 'Gifts of the Spirit' and their application.

Prayer

For born-again believers, prayer is simply talking to Almighty Father God and his Son, the Lord Jesus Christ, in order to make our requests known. To keep it simple here, I will just say prayer can be in the form of petitions or intercessions. Many people 'pray' to false gods e.g. mythological/occultic deities, even dating back to Greek and Roman gods – all usually gods of demonic activity who are opposed to Father God in Heaven, and with Satan, the devil, as their leader, attempt to spread evil/wickedness.

God already knows all about us, even our every thought, but He still loves us. God **is** Love and is ready to hear from us 24/7. Ordinary prayer is talking to God, in a normal voice, using normal decent language, in humility honouring and respecting God as you would if you were talking to a VIP you had longed to talk to. You could compare prayer to talking to your best friend who you really like, respect, and don't want to offend but feel relaxed with, and who allows you to 'be yourself' and say what's on your heart, knowing you're accepted.

It is important to remember to give thanks to God when praying, also to remember that God may give us the answer 'Yes', 'No' or 'Wait' when we bring our requests to Him….we need to remember that **He** is God and **He** knows best!....so we ought to thank Him whatever His answer is!

Prayer can be taking authority in God's power or it can be a desperate cry of the heart, even out loud – see *Psalm 107 verses 6,13,19 and 28*.

Prayer can be petitioning i.e. bringing your 'shopping list' of needs for others and yourself to God, or prayer can be interceding i.e. praying to God for other people{s} and their situation where, as it were, you briefly 'stand in their place', possibly imagining something of how it feels to be in their circumstances, as you cry out to God to help them.

In summary, although there is a lot more to prayer than I've said here, prayer with thanksgiving is a great privilege and can be really **very** helpful.

Hearing God's Voice and How He Does or Might Communicate with us

This is an interesting, vast and complex subject, as God communicates with us in a variety of ways. This is just a brief mention of it here, giving some references, headings and comments to help anyone who may not be aware of this subject and so help to show the bigger picture of it, and hopefully may even be life-changing in its application!

One of the most important ways to live for God in our Christian walk on Earth is through our reading of His Word, the Bible, the Scriptures, consisting of the Old and New Testaments – a total of 66 Books written by various different people who were all inspired by God Himself and so the words written were 'God-breathed'. It is history, 'His-story' of what He {God} was/is doing on this Earth and contains the prophetic writings, the succession of kings, the 'Wisdom Books' e.g. Proverbs, the 'Poetic Books' e.g. Psalms, plus all the different personalities of their time who God wanted us to know about from His Word, both the evil and the good ones. It also contains the sinless, perfect life, death and resurrection of the Lord Jesus, and all the realities of the good and bad sides of life, telling it as it really is, as well as giving character training and training in thanksgiving, prayer and worship. *2 Timothy chapter 3 verse 16* says, 'All Scripture is inspired by God....' and, again, *2 Peter chapter 1 verse 21* tells us '.... but holy men of God spoke as they were moved by the Holy Spirit'.

There are now a great many versions of the Bible, I think over a hundred, some better than others so it is a 'must' to read a reliable version in modern language {based on a sound translation from the original Hebrew Old Testament and Greek New Testament} like the new King James Version {NKJV} or the New International Version {NIV} rather than a suspect 'translation' or paraphrase or a theologically liberal version! Just as a diet of wholesome, healthy food is good for you, so reading a good version of the Bible to 'tune into God' is the spiritually healthy 'Bread of Life' needed for growth and maturity in the things of God and of His Heaven, of life down here on Earth and, of course, of life's other side.

As I've already said, God knows our every thought and every word we've ever spoken and He knows His own Word, the Bible, from beginning to end, so He is fully able to drop into our mind, at any moment, or in any circumstance, exactly what we may need to help us in any situation. Some, like myself, would call this a 'Now Word' from God, especially when desperately asking Him for help. Also, when reading in the Scriptures for His help, a word or phrase, which is totally relevant, sort of 'jumps out from the page' as it were, into one's mind/heart bringing confirmation or help as needed. If this is from God then, in time, it turns out to be a correct 'Now Word' giving the necessary help.

Here is my non-exhaustive list of other ways in which God may speak to any one of us:

{Within the list of God's gifts, which I've previously written about in brief, e.g. prophecy, there are some ways through which God may communicate with us.}

Prophecy – this is very important and if you receive prophecy, given personally/directly to you, it needs to be tested by friends, or Church Leaders you know and trust, regarding its authenticity and regarding what the Word of God says on the subject. The same would apply to a prophecy given out in a Church meeting.

Words of Knowledge

Words of Wisdom

Tongues, Interpretation of Tongues

Discernment

Angelic Appearances i.e. the ministering angels sent to us by God – see *Hebrews chapter 1 verse 14*

Miraculous Happenings e.g. a hand suddenly appeared and wrote on the wall in the king's palace telling the king that his kingdom was finished....and that very night the king was slain! *Daniel chapter 5 verses 5 and 6.*

The Audible Voice of God

Many years ago, I spoke with someone who told me he had heard the audible voice of God. He was mature in the things of God and I believed him.

See: *Psalm 29 verse 3* 'the voice of God thunders'; *Job chapter 37 verse 5* 'God thunders marvellously with His voice'; *Acts chapter 9 verses 3-7* where the Lord Jesus {after His ascension to Heaven} spoke to Saul on his way to Damascus; *John chapter 12 verses 27-30*, another instance of God's voice sounding like thunder then in *1 Kings chapter 19 verses 12 and 13* God spoke to Elijah in a still, small voice {'a gentle whisper'}. These are only some examples of the 'Audible Voice of God' given in Scripture.

Our Circumstances – time to pause or think, 'What is God saying to me or doing in my life?'

Times of Testing – see, for example, *Hebrews chapter 12, 1 Corinthians chapter 10 verse 13, James chapter 1 verse 3*.

Through loving Correction – not punishment but, rather, God correcting us because He loves us

Dreams and Visions – dreams are for the older people in their sleep, and visions {pictures given to people when they are awake} are for the younger people given during daytime. This is a very general viewpoint so there will be some overlap. There are lots of dreams and visions in the Bible as a whole and some of them are very significant and important e.g. Joseph's dream in *Matthew chapter 1 verse 20* and Peter's vision in *Acts chapter 10 verses 9-16*.

Personal Revelation from God e.g. God miraculously revealing to His people what their enemies were plotting against them. In *2 Kings chapter 6 verse 12* we read of Elisha, the Prophet in Israel, being able to report to the King of Israel the very words spoken by the King of Syria in his bedroom, in his plot against the King of Israel, because God revealed the conversation to Elisha!

God Can Even Speak Through A Donkey! See *Numbers chapter 22 verses 21-39* for the account of unrighteous Balaam who was against God. God was so angry with him that He spoke to him, in an audible voice, through his {Balaam's} donkey and a conversation took place leading to Balaam wanting to kill his donkey, at which point the donkey {enabled by God} spoke to Balaam asking him a question which challenged him. Balaam appeared not to 'bat an eyelid' at the fact that his donkey spoke to him but the end result was that he, knowing he was in the wrong, responded to the correction God was giving him. I believe that God has got 'His donkeys' and will speak through them, if needs be, to His own people....so beware, for I reckon God has a sense of humour!

Information regarding both in and around The Tribulation

As I write now about The Tribulation then The Millennium {please see Diagram 2 then Diagram 3} you may remember that I have already covered some of this under the 'plan and purpose' of God .... so, although there may be some overlap it is all important and, I trust, complementary!

As you look at and view the detail of Diagram 2 the important question is, "How do we get from the time we are now in, at the very end of the Age of Grace, to, and through, the 7 year Tribulation {trouble} period to the other side and immediately into the Millennium Age, God's Shabbat or, if you like, our Sunday {Rest Day}?" This will turn out to be the most incredible time on Earth, both good and bad, depending where you stand with the Lord, as there will be a series of happenings just before, or just as, The Tribulation starts........ one could liken The Tribulation to the 3rd World War for a duration of just under 7 years! The 'Heavenly Spotlight', as it were, will go onto the Jews, Israel, and their Land. Immediately {a second} before The Tribulation the true Church {all born-again believers}, worldwide, will be instantly taken out of the equation .... removed to Heaven... {*1 Thessalonians chapter 4 verse 17* in its context}. Satan will fill the void by ruling {with his demons} from the Middle East in the form of the Antichrist i.e. one pretending to be The Christ. Satan wants everybody to accept 'the chip' {or similar} but he is unable to take away one's freedom of choice to refuse it! Again, I urge you to refuse it! Acceptance of it makes it impossible to be born again.

Satan, God's arch-enemy, will rule with full power and control, with a cruelty of death and destruction....there will be unrestrained evil because Father God's love and Holy Spirit through The Messiah, in a general sense, will be taken away to Heaven.....an unbelieving world does not want all that God has to offer. On an individual basis, but only for those who have **not** accepted the 666 'chip' {or whatever that turns out to be} it will still be possible to cry out to God and get saved.... but probably at an enormous personal cost! I believe 'the chip', or whatever, will be a way of numbering everyone on Earth and having all their details on computer, and that **without** 'the chip', in the cashless society it will be, one would be unable to either buy or sell, could have a very rough time, may even be martyred but, having become a believer, would go to Heaven to be with the Trinity of God, all believers and the angels {who did not rebel, so are still in that awesome, beautiful place}.

NOW is the time to cry out to God for Salvation and avoid the horror of the unrestrained evil of the Antichrist in The Tribulation.

God has given us some detail regarding the Earth's time of 7 years of Tribulation. Daniel, a Jew who was in exile along with many other Jews, was mightily used by God as a Prophet. The Old Testament Book of Daniel gives a little clear insight into the time and detail of The Tribulation stating how The Tribulation is in two halves and gives the number of days in each of the three and a half years etc. It is interesting to note that John the Baptist was given three and a half years for his ministry before he was murdered and the Lord Jesus also was given, by Father God, three and a half years of ministry before being crucified. A new temple will be built in Jerusalem, I believe, at the beginning of The Tribulation and the second three and a half years will be worse than the first.

Matthew chapter 24 is very important as the Lord Jesus, there, tells us about The Tribulation, stating very clearly that it will be the worst time ever on Earth in Mankind's history. {The forces of evil will have the boundaries of the old Roman Empire and will be just as cruel or even more cruel than they were in the time of Jesus. See *Daniel chapters 2 and 7* and *Revelation chapters 17 and 18*.}

The main discourse, of course, is found in the Biblical Book of *Revelation*. The whole Book of Revelation was given by the Lord Jesus to, and through, the Apostle John when he was in exile on the Island of Patmos. It is the last preaching or discourse the Lord Jesus gave to His followers and Mankind until He sorts things out pertaining to this time in and around The Tribulation.

Chapter 1 of Revelation deals with the Lord Himself in all His Glory, then come the chapters on His Church {all the true, born again believers} here on Earth. At the start of *chapter 4* the Church and other believers {i.e. as far as I understand, the Old Testament believers later known as friends of the Bridegroom} are all seen in Heaven then the word 'Church' is not mentioned again in Revelation because the Bride {formerly the Church on Earth} is married to the Bridegroom {the Lord Jesus Christ}. The marriage mirrors a Jewish wedding at the time on Earth of Jesus Messiah, from the betrothal to living in the Bridegroom's Father's domain. From then on what was formerly known as 'the Church' became known as 'the Bride'.

What is given in the whole main body of Revelation is an account of all the terrible things that will happen on this Earth, many horrific judgements being poured out on the Earth by God through His angels and most of Mankind will not survive it. *Revelation chapter 13* is important as it shows what the Antichrist is up to on Earth as he 'reigns'....there will be no mercy, no justice, no love, in fact there will be nothing good – there will just be the enemies of God in their wrath.

I will now deal with the section at the very end of the Age of Grace.... this is what I believe anyway after nearly 50 years, on and off, studying the whole subject of Eschatology, the doctrine of the Last Things/End Times. When I was younger I was once well-read and taught by different teachers including those during my time of studying at a popular British Bible College. Around 1983 I was introduced to the teaching of {the now late} Roger Price who was a world leader in many subjects and not least in some of his teaching on Eschatology with his much personal/Biblical revelation from Above. His work is still available as CDs at: www.ccftapes.co.uk and it certainly helped me to get the full picture as I added it to what I had learned over the years.

Please see diagram 2. I will now give a list of mine, of events that will happen just before and around the time of The Tribulation starting, plus some comments. See *Daniel chapter 12 verse 4* - a clear sign of the End Times. *Daniel chapter 12 verses 7-9* shows clearly 2 x 3 and a half years of Tribulation. {A 'time' is one year.}

A. Damascus

B. Jews, the Land of Israel given to them, and their return to Israel

C. Latter Rain Revival

D. Russia

E. Catching away of the Church up into the Heavenlies

F. The Antichrist is revealed {See D [Russia] for further info. re Antichrist.}

G. Further information (from the Book of Revelation) on the Tribulation, to its end, and on into The Millennium {See relevant info. re Tribulation and Millennium elsewhere in the book, also see Diagrams 2 and 3.}

A. Damascus

Damascus has yet to be dealt with by God, in His judgement, for its terrible evil in the Syrian War because of the likes of 'barrel bombs' being dropped on mainly innocent people, both old and young, whose blood cries out to God from the Earth. One day, in Heaven, all the truth will come out - and it will be horrific e.g. what Syria and Russia did.... in fact, all those of the parties involved with dictatorship, with military might under them, including Syria, Russia and Iran, no doubt with others from terrorist organisations they were working with will pay a very high price! It is bad news that Syria has a large store of chemical and biological weaponry. The book of *Isaiah chapter 17* clearly tells us that Damascus will be dealt with and those 'in the know' i.e. Biblical historians, have agreed that this has not yet happened despite Damascus just lying empty at times in its past history. The prophecy in Isaiah will be proven true when no person or creature of any kind will be able to enter Damascus and remain alive. I thought that this would happen this side of the start of The Tribulation but realise now that it might actually belong to the early part of the time of Tribulation... but that it **will** happen is certain – it will be in God's timing and in His way.

Please note that God has given much of the Land of Syria to the Jews, so it is actually part of Israel.

B. The Jews, Israel and their Entire Land

As stated above, the Jews and Israel are God's 'Lead Nation' and are very special to Him. The second The Tribulation starts the spotlight of God, as it were, goes back on to Israel. God will allow certain things to happen on Earth as severe judgement and He will deal with the nations still left at the end of The Tribulation (see below). He, God, of course, will still have the title deeds to Planet Earth, and will allocate as He wills to do so…. it is God's priority to give back the land mass which He has already allocated to the Jews, including Jerusalem.

There are several Scriptures that deal with this which I will list here and I will mention what I believe is the area of land promised by God to the Jews as the Land of Israel… no-one else, even in the Tribulation time, will get a look in regarding laying claim to the land and, of course, it will belong to the Jews and Israel throughout The Millennium. Jerusalem is important, not least because, as The Tribulation starts, a new temple for Jesus the Messiah will be built on the Temple Mount. I believe that Jerusalem, in this present time, is to God, as the Centre of the Universe. Please note, as in the book of Revelation, for the Eternal State, there will be a New Earth, a New Heaven and a New Jerusalem etc.

Here is a short list of some of the Bible references related to the 'Land of Israel': *Genesis chapter 15 verse 18*; *Genesis chapter 17 verse 8*; *Exodus chapter 23 verse 31*; *Ezekiel chapter 47 verses 13 to 20*.

I believe that this is from the Euphrates River down to, and including, the Red Sea, also including the Great River which is the River Nile and from the Jordan River over to the Mediterranean which includes all of what was the Land of Canaan, Gaza and so much of what was the Land of Syria and is a vast area. God will see to it that it is given to the Jews according to His promises in Scripture and that no-one else from anywhere will be given it or dwell in it on a permanent basis.

Things will be going on in Jerusalem but the Antichrist will not win in any way against the Jews overall. See below, at the end of The Tribulation when Jesus returns to Earth, He will then sort out all the 'Sheep Nations' and 'Goat Nations' so that the 'Sheep Nations' can go into the Millennium Age.

I used to think that all the Jews from around the Earth would go to live in the Land of Israel before the start of The Tribulation - it could still happen as a miracle of God - but I now think that at the very early part of The Tribulation God may cause all of the Jews to go to what will be the entire God-given Land of Israel.

C. The Latter Rain Revival

What I'm about to say depends on the fact that God owes us 9 of Earth's days as clearly shown in the early part of the Book of Acts. Please see below for an explanation of this. I say this could be 4 days for a very powerful Latter Rain Revival followed by 5 days for Russia's military might to reach the Middle East and be wiped out by God.

In the Middle East the latter rain is a powerful deluge of water given to swell out the harvest. Revival is a powerful deluge of Holy Spirit poured out on Earth to swell a harvest of whatever God wants to help Mankind with, or to swell out 'a harvest of souls' into His Kingdom. A God-given revival can last days, weeks, months or even years. God can do anything He wants, it is no problem for Him to have the most powerful outpouring of His Holy Spirit right round Planet Earth for say 4 of Earth's days, in which many will be saved, healed and helped, as need be, to swell out the harvest of souls to a number that He, God the Father, wants for Heaven, as the first part of those 9 days.

Explanation re the 9 days owed to Mankind

To give understanding to this …. there are, in the Book of Acts, two key verses in their context. Firstly, in *Acts chapter 1 verse 3* we have the key word 'forty' "… being seen by them during **forty** days …." – He, Jesus, was very busy speaking of the Kingdom of God, telling the people He was the Messiah and what He'd been through for them. Secondly, in *Acts chapter 2 verse 1*, we have the key word 'fully' – "When the Day of Pentecost had **fully** come…" The word 'fully' in this context means the 50th day.

Pentecost is the Baptism of the Holy Spirit upon Jesus's disciples in Jerusalem on the 50th day after the Jewish Feast of Passover, so take away from 50 the 40 days that Jesus was ministering and that leaves 10 days. The Jewish Festival of Passover is actually held on the 50th day after the **second** day of Passover, so it is not, in fact, 50 days from Passover to Pentecost but actually only 49 days.

Jesus ministered powerfully for 40 days *(Acts chapter 1 verse 3)* of those 49 days from Passover to Pentecost so 9 days are still unaccounted for, therefore owed to us by God. I believe that those 9 days, due to us, of powerful ministry by the Lord Jesus, will most likely be 4 days of an incredible revival overseen by Jesus Himself, then 5 days of all the Russian military might on its way to the Middle East to destroy whatever, then the Lord making sure that Russia itself is taken out of the equation!

D. Russia

I believe (as stated in section C above) that the second part of the 9 days, just before The Tribulation starts, involves Russia, that rogue, terrible nation which wants to take over the world. It loves to show off its military might and so it will gather together its military might, go to the Middle East, no doubt intent on gaining a strong foothold for itself and be determined to wipe out Israel and all the Jews, taking their Land for itself. Russia is a ruthless nation and as its military might goes down to the Middle East, which could easily take only 5 days, it will destroy anything and everything in its way.... but when it gets there **it** will be destroyed by God and made useless! At the same time God will deal with all the political leadership in Moscow or wherever - not one will survive. The tape/CD in Roger Price's series on 'Unfulfilled Prophecy' entitled 'Does Russia have a future?' deals with his teaching on this from *Ezekiel chapters 38 and 39*. If you live to see this unfolding before your eyes you will be aware that the moment it is finished happening will be the very moment that all true Christians worldwide, many millions of people, will be, in just a second of time, removed from the Earth as prophesied in *1 Thessalonians chapter 4 verse 17*.

Within a second of the above is the exact time that the Antichrist, who is around, will be allowed to take up his place by coming forward to start the Tribulation time with his deceptive, evil ways. He will, along with signs and wonders, pretend to have all the answers and so many peoples of the Earth, looking for a leader, will think he is the Messiah and will follow him.

I believe (see earlier writing) that the 666 in *Revelation chapter 13* could be a computer chip which will be able to number all the people of the Earth who have agreed to have a tiny chip implanted in their right hand or forehead, leaving a mark, the so-called 'mark of the beast' (*Revelation chapter 13*) and all the various personal details of those with the chip will be available to those who serve the Antichrist. To recap what I wrote previously, it is just like a chip put into an animal, only in humans it will leave a mark! People will be living in a cashless society and the only way to buy or sell anything will be via the chip. The group of numbers, I would say, will enable identification by computer, of every place and every person on Earth. The Antichrist will not require anyone to speak on his behalf but, as a terrible dictator, he will work by coercive control with his vast and ruthless armies, along with all his demons and those who have accepted the chip. The extent of evil will be horrific and all the talk being bandied about now in 2020, regarding awful things happening in science labs, which currently sound like science fiction e.g. changing of human genetic codes, might well be possible... keeping to the content of the book of Revelation, especially chapter 13, is enough! The time is short and the devil/Antichrist can only do so much and go no further!

E. Catching Away of the Church up into the Heavenlies

Firstly, Russia, with its military might, when it gets to the Middle East, will be dealt with by God. Immediately after that the Church worldwide will be instantaneously caught away into the Heavenlies (in and above the clouds) to join all those from the Age of Grace who will have come down, just at that time, from Paradise in Heaven (but **not** right down to Earth) with the Lord Jesus. All the believers still on Earth will be caught up to join all those in the air, in and above the clouds with the Lord Jesus (see *1 Thessalonians chapter 4 verse 17*) and will all go off to Heaven with the Lord Jesus. As stated above they are going to a wedding... the marriage of what was formerly the Church, now, many millions of believers as the Bride, to the Messiah, Lord Jesus, as the Bridegroom, with 7 'days' of wedding ceremony and celebration at the Father's place which was the format of a Jewish Wedding of 2000 years ago.

The above is often referred to as 'The Rapture' although this word, from its Latin origin, does not appear, as such, in the Bible. If you wish to study this further then doing some research into the Greek words 'Parousia' and 'Harpazo' would be helpful regarding understanding *1 Thessalonians chapter 4 verses 17 and 18* ... 'the snatching away of the Church' and 'being in the presence of the Lord forever'.

To spell it out .... while this wedding with its celebrations is taking place in Heaven, The Tribulation will be taking place on Earth and, as already stated, the length of its time will be just less than 7 years.

F. The Antichrist is Revealed

Please see section D above

G. Further Information on Tribulation {from Book of Revelation} to its end, and on into The Millennium

The main body of the Book of Revelation consists of details of The Tribulation time - it is horrific! At the end of The Tribulation most of the Earth's population will be dead. From the East, a great military army will march down to the Middle East, no doubt to try to take over the Middle East and destroy Israel and the Jews. This army, I believe, will be Chinese, as China wants to take over the whole world (as did Russia previously). I believe some of India's military might will be included in this army, possibly along with that of one or two other countries. It must be many millions in strength. When they reach the Middle East the world will be, by then, in terrible turmoil with Mankind wanting to destroy each other - they can't destroy the Earth itself but God will do that later from the centre of the Earth outwards. At this point this massive army will be destroyed by God at the Battle of Armageddon in the Valley of Megiddo in Israel - the worst ever battle for Mankind!

At this very time the Lord Jesus must return to Earth in order to save Mankind from total self-destruction. The Trinity of God will bring to an end the Antichrist's rule on Earth and prepare for the Millennium Age. Satan will be put, in the spiritual world, into a bottomless pit for 1000 years.

Now is the time that the Lord Jesus will sort out all the remaining nations of the Earth, large or small, and divide them into 'goat groups' of peoples or nations and 'sheep groups'. The 'goat nations/peoples' are those who are opposed to God and they will be taken out into the Heavenly realm to await their everlasting fate away from God in the Lake of Fire prepared for the devil, the beast and the false prophet and all the fallen angels with them. The 'sheep nations and groups of peoples' will stay on Earth to go into the Millennium Age of God's Rest Day for Earth, to populate the Earth for 1000 years. People will generally live all the way through the Millennium Age. As God is in total control He will just give the words and the whole Earth will be transformed into perfection – all the mess Mankind has made with plastic etc. will be gone - all will be put right by God. There will be no work to do, no money, every need well provided for. Food for Mankind and animals will be easily accessible - there will be no need to cultivate the land, no labour, no weeds, fruit available to pick from trees, animals all friendly and peaceful - God's provision of everything necessary for Mankind and animals. The weather will be perfect all the time, all people and animals well fed by what God allows to grow, no lack of any kind, no challenges as such … sounds wonderful … but the strange thing is that despite living in this superb environment where one might expect people to tune in to the Lord Jesus and go to see Him and talk with Him, where He will be available in the Temple in Jerusalem, there will be no 'takers' and, not only this, but at the end of 1000 years of perfection Mankind will choose to cry out for Satan! In response the Trinity of God will release Satan from the bottomless pit back onto Earth and Satan, in order to destroy whatever, will lead the people further in their rebellion against the Lord Jesus who has been in the Temple in Jerusalem throughout The Millennium. At that point God will say (my words) 'Enough is enough! I have proved my point – it's now all over!' He will have given Mankind absolute perfection, everything wonderful for His Rest Day of 1000 years but Mankind will still not want the Trinity of God with all that is offered to them… all they will want is Satan, so God will give them what they choose! There is no record of any believers on Earth at that time.

Diagram 2

From the end of the Age of Grace and Mercy to the start of the 1000 years of God's perfect 'Rest Day' Millennium Age for Mankind .... centred on the time just leading up to The Tribulation period of just under 7 Earth years and The Tribulation (trouble) itself

End of the
2000 years
of God's Grace

This gap here is when the true Messiah returns to Earth to draw to a close the Battle of Armageddon, put a stop to Satan's rule on Earth until the very end of The Millennium and sort out the 'goat and sheep nations' with only the 'sheep nations' going into the Millennium Age to repopulate the Earth.

↓

This is the very end of the Age of God's Grace and Mercy

The 7 of Earth's years of terrible trouble in 2 x 3 and a half years

The start of the 1000 years of God's 'Rest Day' for Mankind, The Millennium

(See Daniel ch 12 verse 4 and verses 7-9 ... A 'time' is one year)

See Diagram 3 etc

(See G below and other info in this book about The Tribulation)

See A to G below

↓

This is what I think will happen around the beginning of The Tribulation .... 7 things - the timing of some is uncertain to us, see info from A to G, as listed fully in this book.

A Damascus

B The Jews and Israel are again the centre of God's attention

C The Latter Rain Revival in 4 of the 9 days owed to us by God

D Russia is dealt with by God in 5 of the 9 days owed to us by Him

E God supernaturally takes the true Church worldwide 'out of the equation' in a second of time to be with Him in the Heavenlies and, of course, forever.

F The moment E, just above, happens the Antichrist starts his despotic, deceitful rule on Earth for just under 7 years.

G The main body of the book of *Revelation is, I would say, from chapter 5 to 16*, on the one hand, God's anger of judgements, woes and plagues on an unbelieving Mankind and, … on the other hand, Satan, the devil, ruling on Earth so that means there is deep trouble for Mankind coming from both God above and from Satan ruling on Earth! Satan's plan is, through pure evil, to totally control Mankind*. This will be the worst time ever on Earth – Mankind will be decimated!

Revelation chapter 13 and *Matthew chapter 24*, as previously stated, are both important. *Revelation chapter 16 verse 16* refers to the greatest, most terrible battle on Earth, which I believe will involve a major part of Chinese military might plus others - this is when the Lord Jesus will have to come to Earth to deal with things to stop Mankind from wiping itself out - so The Tribulation will be cut short. All the main armies at this Battle of Armageddon will be destroyed. This battle will take place on the vast Plain of Megiddo in Israel - I have been there and have seen the area - a very moving experience as I 'soaked it in'. Although I have read *Revelation chapters 5 to 16* I have never done an in-depth study of it. There are other things dealt with in Revelation too but the above is enough for this book!

*(He wants to manipulate Mankind so as to negate even one of God's promises in the Bible by altering what God has said would happen to all of Mankind during their time on Earth, thus trying to make God a liar, so that he, Satan, could stay on Earth forever…. but this will never happen…. God is all powerful and He is Truth!)

Great White Throne Judgement

Revelation chapter 20 verses 11-15

Next comes the Great White Throne Judgement in Heaven - see Diagram 3. This is the final Judgement Seat of God in Heaven. It will be presided over by the Messiah, i.e. the Lord Jesus, who will sit on the Great White Throne and will judge every being who has ever lived apart from all the angelic beings in Heaven who did not rebel against God when tested by Satan, the devil. {Please note that all the people who were alive on Earth at the end of The Millennium and asked for, and got, the devil, in order to come against Jerusalem and the Messiah in the Temple, to destroy them, were dealt with by Father God with fire from Heaven and were all wiped out and, with the devil, were immediately cast into the Lake of Fire and Brimstone forever for all their terrible wrong-doing, in spite of God being so kind to them during the whole 1000 years of The Millennium. They were judged instantly by God because their sin was so apparent and horrific and that is why they do not appear at the Great White Throne Judgement - their obvious and just fate was given to them by Father God, in powerful judgement, at that moment of time.}

At the Great White Throne Judgement everything ever said and done by Mankind, as individuals, will be made known and all secrets will be revealed. Everyone, in all of Mankind, will be justly sentenced to either Heaven or Hell depending on whether they chose God or not while they were alive on Earth and if they didn't choose the Trinity of God they will be separated from Him and all that He is, forever and ever.

Everyone will know where they are going for all eternity and everyone will realise that this has been a totally fair and right judgement by God. The separation from God for those who have not chosen Him must be dreadful as they will, by then, never be able to call on the name of the Lord and get saved. For all those who, while alive on Earth, did choose Father God, with all that He offered, it will be fully about worshipping, thanking and praising Him in and for His love, forever ...... just like a powerful revival meeting here on Earth, multiplied at least a million times I would guess! This will be in an amazing, incredibly beautiful place of a New Heaven, New Earth, New Jerusalem, River of Life etc. etc., with streets of pure gold, marvellous colours, glorious music, magnificent jewels ......unspeakable joy of being face to face with the Lord Jesus, with the light emanating from Him being our light forever in an eternal day, basking in His love everywhere..... it is beyond description!!

All those who have chosen the Lord Jesus in the Age of Grace will have their names written in Jesus, the Lamb of God's Book of Life and will live for all eternity, forever and ever, in this perfect, absolutely wonderful environment built by Father God and He, God, will dwell in the New Zion, at the New Jerusalem..... Glory!! (All Old Testament believers, as I understand it, who lived before the Age of Grace and Mercy, will also be in Heaven for all eternity and are classed as 'Friends of the Bridegroom'. Their names are written in the 'Book of Life', as I have mentioned elsewhere in this book.)

After the Great White Throne Judgement is over the present Earth will be totally destroyed, from within to the outside, by God - gone completely - and the Universe will be all closed down - the Bible tells us it will be like a cloth/cloak/robe rolled up and put away by God *{Hebrews chapter 1 verses 10-12}*.

Sadly, all of the fallen angelic beings and all of Mankind who did not want all that Father God had so lovingly done for them, will be put in the Lake of Fire, along with Satan and his minions, forever and ever, totally separated from those in Heaven.

In Heaven, beautifully called by some 'THE ETERNAL STATE' there will be no tears, no pain, no sadness, no sickness, no sin of any kind - just absolute perfection forever and ever in this unimaginably beautiful place.

I know that reading all of this could be very painful for some, but the reality is that once you get to life's other side i.e. when you die, it's too late to change your mind .... the choice is yours down here on Earth so, please, choose to accept the wonderful gift given by God at Calvary's Cross - the gift of Salvation through the Lord Jesus and taste of God's awesome love that will last forever. Please do it now before you're too late. God's indescribable love, care and provision are so worth having at any cost, so cry out to Him and He will hear you - say a prayer to Him, ask Him to help you, give Him your heart, your all, in truth and humility....... so much is at stake.... what have you got to lose? ..... you have so much to gain.... act on this now, live for Him .... you will never regret it!

Diagram 3

From the very end of The Tribulation Time at the battle of Armageddon to the beginning of the Eternal State with emphasis on The Millennium and The Great White Throne Judgement in Heaven

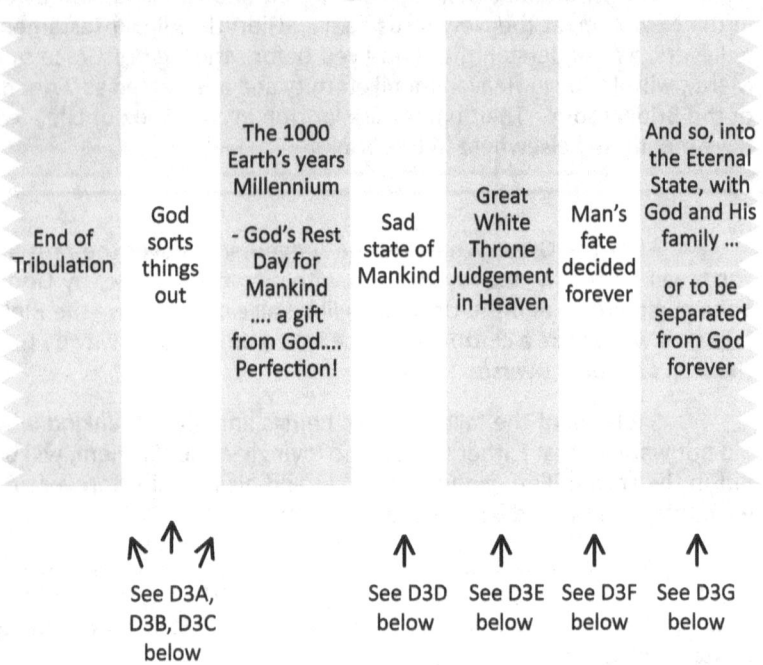

D3A, D3B, D3C

At the end of the terrible Tribulation period, as already covered above, there will be a great army from the East. This can only be from the Godless China which still wants to take over the whole world, and at this point to destroy Israel and the Jews in order to get a foothold in the Middle East from which to carry out its plans. I would say this army will be joined by parts of other armies as well e.g. India, in total many millions, who will gather at the plain of Megiddo where there will take place the worst ever battle in human history, the Battle of Armageddon - truly horrific!

Something will cause the blood of all these military people to be released (could this possibly be nuclear warfare?), indeed all these people may simply turn on each other - the bloodshed will be "as high as horses' bridles" (*Revelation chapter 14 verse 20*).

These vast armies won't touch the rest of Israel but, in order to stop Mankind from destroying itself, the Lord Jesus will have to return to the Earth before the end of The Tribulation (we are not told in Scripture how long in time that is). The Lord Jesus, with the angelic armies of Heaven, will bring to an end this Battle of Armageddon. A massive earthquake will occur which will reach from there to at least Jerusalem and the armies of Armageddon (see *Revelation chapter 16 verse 16*) will be destroyed and it will be all over for the forces of evil at that time. This must happen and the Lord Jesus will take up residence in the new Temple in Jerusalem where there will be a new river flowing from His Throne. Satan, the devil, will be cast into the bottomless pit for 1000 years, the time of the Millennium Age.

The Lord Jesus will stay in the Temple in Jerusalem and prepare and clean up everything on Earth for the Millennium - a perfect, clean environment across the board where every need will be provided for. The Trinity of God will sort it all out as needs be - the climate will be perfect! Food will be readily available, everything will be relaxing, effortless and perfect for Mankind, no weeds or contamination anywhere - it is God's 'Rest Day' - no work for anyone! There are Scriptures in Isaiah re the perfect harmony and peace there will be. (e.g. *Isaiah chapter 11 verses 6-9* and *chapter 65 verse 25*)

The Lord Jesus will put all the peoples still remaining on the Earth into 'sheep nations' (**for** God) and 'goat nations' (**against** God). The latter will be removed from the Earth, to be justly dealt with, and the former will stay to populate the Earth, as stated, in and for The Millennium. The Lord Jesus will be available to talk with anyone in the Jerusalem Temple during the Millennium!

D3D

At the very end of The Millennium, after all that God has done to share with Mankind His 'Day of Rest', the Earth's population will cry out, not for the Trinity of God but for the devil, Satan! Now we know that God may choose to give you what you so desperately want or cry out for, good or bad, so God will release the devil from the bottomless pit where he will have been throughout the Millennium Age and Satan will immediately get the people together to go to the Temple in Jerusalem with a view to destroying whatever - but at that point God will say {my words}, 'No! That is enough!' and the devil, with all his followers, will be cast into the Lake of Fire and Brimstone, forever ... see *Revelation chapter 20 verses 7-10*.

When I first understood all this I was looking for 'the believers' from out of The Millennium and as I couldn't manage to find any record of them in Scripture I thought I had failed and 'lost the plot' ....but, there aren't any!! The late Roger Price in, I think, his 'Millennium CDs' {the only person I've ever heard who} clearly stated that there will be no believers in the Lord God coming out of The Millennium! Despite all of God's perfection in His provision for Mankind at that time there are no takers - very sad!!

Strangely, although Scripture clearly tells us of a literal 1000 year 'Millennium Age' on Earth, with the Lord Jesus living in Jerusalem, the subject, in my experience over many years, does not appear to be preached on or taught.

D3E

The Great White Throne Judgement will take place in Heaven and Jesus, the Saviour, Messiah, King of kings and Lord of lords will be fully in charge of the Kingdom of Heaven, as Judge, with authority given to Him by the Father God - all proceedings will be totally fair, kind, just and righteous. All Mankind will be judged and each man's fate will be decided forever - either to be with God in His Heaven or to be separated from God in the Lake of Fire, that place so terrible, prepared for the devil and fallen angels . . . . and fallen man who did not want God will go there as well forever. These people will not be able to cry out to the Trinity of God for Salvation - that is the way God has made it!

So, at the Judgement in Heaven, we will all, individually, have to give an account for every wrong or empty word we have ever uttered, all of our sins, our secret sins, our deceptive thoughts and actions, our breaking of the Mosaic Ten Commandments and, no doubt, the Lord will show specific sins to individuals if He has to.

All who have believed in God and the finished work of the Lord Jesus and whose sins are covered by His shed Blood, i.e. all who are born again, have their sins forgiven. They will go with God to His Heaven to be with Him and His Family in an incredibly beautiful place to worship, praise, love, thank {etc.} Him forever.

This Judgement is found in *Revelation chapter 20 verses 11 – 15*. The key to this is simply stated - there are Books in Heaven and one of them is mentioned in *Revelation chapter 20 verse 15* - it is 'The Book of Life' and only those who have their names in that Book, through their love relationship with God, will go to Heaven. See also in *Revelation chapter 21 verse 27* 'The Lamb's Book of Life' - the same applies as to 'The Book of Life'. The 'Lamb's Book of Life' {in my understanding} contains the names of New Testament believers.

D3F and D3G

These two diagram sections, at the end of diagram 3, I will briefly deal with, as one 'seen together', and I need to mention first the relevant Bible references for them {especially clear in the New King James Version which I like reading}. I will give the Bible references only and not the actual quotations from Revelation, the last Book of the Bible, which clearly reveals future events.

Revelation chapter 16 verse 16 …. Armageddon is mentioned

Revelation chapter 19 verse 20 …. God's archenemies are eternally dealt with by God

Revelation chapter 20 verses 7-10 …. This is at the end of the 1000-year Age, Satan is released from the bottomless pit, he deceives the nations and he and the nations surround Jerusalem. God sends fire from Heaven to devour them, His enemies, and the devil {verse 10} is immediately cast into the Lake of Fire and Brimstone to join the other parts of the Satanic Trinity - the Beast and the False Prophet. The demons {fallen angels who rebelled against God and followed Satan from Heaven} are cast into the Lake of Fire around this time.

Revelation chapter 20 verses 11-15 makes clear the reality of the Great White Throne Judgement in Heaven with the Messiah, Jesus, as King and Judge. Verse 15 mentions the 'Book of Life' and another similar verse, *Revelation chapter 21 verse 27*, tells of the 'Lamb's Book of Life'.

These two Books are extremely important because only all the people whose names are written in either one or the other of these Books are going to Heaven …. and so it is that every person whose name is not written in one of these Books of Life, after the Great White Throne Judgement, will be cast into the Lake of Fire.

Revelation chapter 21 verses 1-5 …. The first Earth and first Heaven are destroyed by God and are completely gone.

Revelation chapter 21 tells us that a new Earth, new Heaven and a new Jerusalem, the Holy City, come down from God out of Heaven. Note, there is no more sea because it is not needed {as a cleansing agent} in Heaven because Heaven is totally clean.

Revelation chapter 21 verses 1-5 and *verses 9-27* is a wonderful and important passage of Scripture for it describes all about the Heavenly State of the New Jerusalem, God's Domain from Heaven, the New Earth and the New Jerusalem. It is incredibly beautiful. The late Roger Price made a CD on this subject entitled 'The Eternal State' and it is so good it left me almost speechless! …. A 'must' to listen to!

Revelation chapter 22 is also very relevant as it speaks of the River of Life and it shows the beauty of the Lord and of His Heaven. God has sorted it all out …. The old has gone and the **new** has come, forever …. This **new** {currently in the future, as I write now in December 2020, while we're still living at the end of the Age of Grace} is the unspeakably beautiful Eternal State!

The next major event for all true believers is the 'Catching Away of the Church' worldwide. Diagram 2 refers to events between now, 2020, and the 'Catching Away'.

Revelation chapter 22, the last chapter of the Bible, tells us clearly that the Lord wants to comfort and help us by letting us know He's coming back soon and there will be just rewards given by Him {*Revelation chapter 22 verse 12*} …. so, I beg you, while you still have the freedom to do so, to make sure that **your** name is written in Jesus the Lamb's Book of Life so that **you** {and, through you, your children who have not yet reached the age of accountability [*2 Samuel chapter 12 verse 23, 1 Corinthians chapter 7 verses 12-15*] …. God knows those who are His} will be in a loving relationship with the Lord Jesus, His Father God and the Holy Spirit, in the absolutely beautiful and wonderful Eternal State, forever!!!

Appendix

1.
Henry A Field
Born in Newcastle upon Tyne towards end of 2nd World War

I have written my autobiography 'The Way I See It'
ISBN: 978-1-905553-63-1

Published in 2010 by Dolman Scott, still available online
(but unfortunately sometimes advertised wrongly as if written by Henry F Field)

Comments about 'The Way I See It'

… it has the potential to change your life for the better as you allow it to do so…

… it is meant to challenge you as in think, search, and ask questions for the meaning and reality of life itself… even in all its joys, trials and tribulations… and to consider life's other side… and reach out for God's love to you…

… so the book is written to speak to and help those who want to put things right with the Lord God… the main part of the book is taken up with my autobiography to show where I'm coming from for I've seen and experienced much… wealth and poverty… rejection… spouse bereavement… divorce… some horrific boarding schools in my earlier years… parental violence in my upbringing… incest in my first wife's family… many adventures… the importance of warfare as in good versus evil, that includes some amazing accounts from the Second World War etc. etc.

Feedback and Reviews

Lee, Northumberland: …. Henry has a real writing gift that should be used

Marjory, Dumbarton: …. Brill book - love the writing style!

Margherita, Newcastle: …. I am really enjoying reading the book so far and feel I could have been there

Alan, Harrogate: …. Thought there was too much detail

Sheena, Mid-Northumberland: …. Liked the detail

Bill, Glasgow: …. Nearly lost the will to live several times when reading the book

Tony, Folkestone: …. Well done Henry with the book…. for telling it straight…. encouraged by the honesty and 'realness'…. that is carrying on with me…. what a life story…. you've done really well to recall so much detail and convey it so honestly and clearly…. the stuff about cultish fellowships was especially important…. as so many have been hurt and totally put off by heavy shepherding, legalism etc. …. reader friendly…. and a lovely volume.

Dave, Blyth: …. Just got your book, opened it to view…. I'm gripped! …. fascinating, compelling reading so far, it feels like you are face to face telling me the story.

Amy, Cramlington: …. A good book, excellent - I'm going to read it again.

Grace, Northumberland: …. In tears reading the book…. first thing I'm packing in my suitcase to take to my Dad (West Africa).

UK Review 8th October 2012

Johnstrek   5 stars   Interesting read!!!

There is so much that goes on in a lifetime and it's quite interesting to read a normal person's story, the ups and downs that affect us, some of the author's are quite harrowing, all in all great read for the price and I would recommend it if you're fed up of reading biographies of the rich and famous which are 10 a penny!!

Rayking   Revealing   UK Review   12th February 2012   4 stars

A very thought-provoking read, although I have not had any personal experience of the contents, it makes the reader very much aware of the problems that exist in the world.

1a. The Doctrine of The End Times, with regard to God's overall plan, has been one of my favourite subjects from the Bible since the early 1970s when I first learnt about it and I would say it is one of the most rewarding subjects to deal with. It is a difficult and complex subject, as such, though very important. It is necessary for us to get the right structure/skeleton, as it were, on which to build/put flesh because if we don't it will lead to problems.

There is another thing here that is important to get right. People gather together the many verses from Scripture on this subject, and in trying to put them in their right places, they sometimes fail and get it wrong then the 'big picture' is also wrong so it won't make sense overall. If you do put the Scripture verses in their right place, where they fit, then the 'big picture' will make sense. It can take a long time to get to know this vast subject in such a way as to fit it all together correctly... yes, it is rather like a big jigsaw puzzle - each piece must fit exactly in its place to give the proper end result.

1b. The Gospel of *John chapter 3 verses 1-16* .... Nicodemus (I will call him Nic for short in this article)

Nic was an important, leading, religious leader in Israel. Nic had been watching the Lord Jesus for a while and wanted to speak with Him so went, under cover of darkness - if the other Jews he mixed with had known this I believe they would have killed him without mercy as **they** would not have Jesus at any cost! .... So Nic came to Jesus and his words to Jesus were,

'.... for no-one can do these signs that You do unless God is with him'

That was, I believe, Nic saying that Jesus **was** The Messiah the Jews were waiting for. Jesus came straight to the real issue, no messing, *(verse 3)* by replying,

'.... unless one is born again, he cannot **see** the Kingdom of God' .... In other words, Jesus told Nic that he **must** be born again. Nic's answer was deep and profound as he was thinking it through correctly, as seen in his words in *verse 4* .... he was wise, not stupid. The Lord answered him, in *verses 5 to 8*, by explaining that at his birth he had been born of water (when his mother's waters broke, in the natural) but now needed to be born of the Spirit above. Jesus further explained that to be born again of the Spirit from Heaven, i.e. the Holy Spirit, directly into his heart, was what would transform him and change him by bringing him into a relationship with the Trinity of God and His family who belong to Heaven. Jesus told Nic he could not **see** the Kingdom of God unless he **saw** the King i.e. unless Nic **saw**/realised that Jesus **was** the King! ....

So, what do you (as the reader) **see** when you humble yourself before God and ask Him into your heart and life and believe in the Trinity of God? You **see** that the Lord Jesus, Messiah, **is** the King of Heaven, the King of kings and Lord of lords. It follows, that you will be completely changed, from the inside out, by God's love and power and you will **see** the Kingdom of God clearly.... the King will be reigning in your heart from the moment you are born again! If you mean it and trust Him and look to Him, as you believe in Him and His finished work, even just for **you**, you will have joy unspeakable as you will be in relationship with the Trinity of God and so walk with Him and relate to Him, as I have spoken about, as simply as I can, in this book.

A Prayer for Salvation-To know you are going to Heaven

To know God's Love

Henry A. Field

Heavenly Father, Lord Jesus (Yeshua) Christ, Holy Spirit - I may not fully understand at this time, but I acknowledge You as The Trinity of God and believe in You so help me now as I put my trust in You. Please help me as I pray this prayer.

I know I have sinned/done wrong in my thoughts, words and actions. There are so many good things I have not done .... There are so many sinful/wrong things I have done. I am sorry for my sins - please help me and I will turn from everything I know to be wrong. I renounce all religiosity, any and all occult and any cult involvement and ask for Your total cleansing. I yield myself to You - my pride, anger, hurt, pain, selfishness and any bitterness, everything. I give it all to You. Please forgive me. As an act of my will I forgive all others, no matter who, when or where, who have done wrong to me, and break/release the emotional pain of the abuse from me, both conscious and sub-conscious. I forgive myself .... Soul and Body, I forgive you. I give You my guilt, real and perceived. I break off me all wrong inner vows and curses.

As You gave Your life, Lord Jesus, upon The Cross for me, by and through Your sinless, perfect shed blood, and died my death and gave me Your Life - Your blood come into my life and cleanse me from every sin .... Gratefully I give my life back to You and ask You to come into my heart and life as my Lord and King. Come in as my Saviour to cleanse me. Come in as my Lord to control me. Come in as my Friend to be with me. Come in by Your Holy Spirit and flood me and baptise me with Your Holy Spirit Love. I will do my best to love You as You have first loved me, to have a close relationship with You and serve You as You give me the gift to do so. Let me walk in that serving in obedience to You and fellowship with You all my days on Earth.

Thank You and I praise You Lord Jesus that You will take me to Your Heaven to be with You forever. Thank You Heavenly Father that You are now my perfect "Dad" with unconditional love for me. Thank You Holy Spirit that You are my Comforter and much much more. Clean me up, mature me and let me be like You, Lord Jesus. Free me from all demonic activity and teach me in Your Way and let me be Your disciple and a Kingdom of God/Heaven believer/builder.

I confess that Jesus Christ is God and walked in the flesh on this Earth.

Thank You that my Salvation is totally dependent upon You.

JESUS IS LORD! I love You Heavenly Father/Lord Jesus and praise You.

AMEN and AMEN!

1c. You can hardly call the whole Book of Revelation, as such, an easy Book to deal with or come to terms with! As I remember, it was the late Roger Price who said, somewhere in his vast amount of good Bible teaching, that he wanted to do a verse by verse teaching/commentary on the Book of Revelation. He did not live long enough to do that though the groundwork he did cover was excellent. Some have said that the key to understanding the Book of Revelation is to realise that it is full of symbolism - and if you can understand what some of these symbols are, and mean, then it is easier to understand the Book of Revelation. Very briefly, without going into this subject here and now, a quick example of Biblical symbolism in the New Testament can be seen in two things the Lord Jesus gave, while He walked on Earth, for the Church to do. One, was to be baptised as believers, once only, by total immersion (where possible) - symbolizing the death, burial, resurrection and life etc. in Him. The other was The Last Supper (which I call The Lord's Table) where Jesus gave the bread and wine to His disciples, which was symbolic of the sacrifice of His body and shed blood in what He was about to go through for Mankind up to Calvary's Cross and beyond. Jesus told His disciples...and, a little later, through them, the Church, that this was to be done regularly, as often as they would choose to do so, in remembrance of Him and His finished work for Salvation up to Calvary and beyond. (A substitute for alcoholic wine may be used.)

One clear example of symbolism from towards the end of the Book of Revelation is 'the Great Harlot' (*chapter 17 from verse 1*) and it refers to the long gone Babylon which was totally evil and, as I understand it, in Revelation this refers to Rome with all its decadence and materialism and horrific Godlessness, bringing God's fierce anger into the situation. I believe this would tie in with the EU and the Antichrist in The Tribulation and therefore have God's fierce anger and judgement in the situation.

There is much in the Book of Revelation, including the wrath of God constantly poured out on sinful, unbelieving Mankind, in His judgement against all those who do not want Him and what he had, the good things, prepared for them. It has been said that if you take the first three chapters of the Bible i.e. *chapters 1-3 of Genesis*, and the last 3 chapters of the Bible i.e. *Revelation chapters 20-22*, the former will show you where it all went wrong for Mankind and the latter will show you where God sorted it all out, justly.... that is amazing! (I haven't done an in-depth study on this, but it sounds okay to me.)

For a written record of the contents and diagrams in this, my book, regarding what **God** has listed and shown about these End Times, please read the following verses and chapters from the end of the Book of Revelation to show that what I've written is based on, and in line with, God's Word.

Revelation chapter 16 verses 11-14,16 ...all preparation for the great, horrific Battle of Armageddon... *ch 19 v 7-9* ... to do with the Marriage of The Lamb to His Bride in Heaven, formerly the true Church on Earth in the Age of Grace, but now His Bride in Heaven and *v 9* speaks of the Old Testament Believers/Friends of the Bridegroom ... *ch 19 v 17-21* ... refers to the end of The Tribulation and the Battle of Armageddon and *verse 20* is important information about the fate of the Beast and the False Prophet ... *ch 20 v 1-3* ... Satan is bound for 1000 years ... *ch 20 v 7-9* ... refers to the Battle being attempted at the end of The Millennium

... *ch 20 v 10* is the end of the devil as he is cast into the Lake of Fire and Brimstone (Sulphur) and so the Satanic Trinity is, then, there forever and ever ... *ch 20 v 11-15* tells of the Great White Throne Judgement, and all that was not of God was cast into the Lake of Fire and Brimstone forever, all those beings sentenced to the Lake of Fire are now there forever... all those who belong to the Trinity of God go with God to the Eternal State Domain/place of incredible beauty, forever ... *ch 21 v 1,2* ... verses of great importance! - the old has gone and the new has come - the New Jerusalem is where true believers and the Heavenly angelic host, with the Trinity of God, will be forever ... *ch 21 v 3-5* ...begins to give insight as to what Heaven is like and *v 6-9* gives more background info ... *ch 21 v 10-27* shows with detail what the New Jerusalem is like ... it is incredibly wonderful and beautiful beyond words I would say ... (please note, as already referred to, that the late Roger Price's CD, Basic Bible Study [BBS] No 62, entitled 'The Eternal State', is a **must** to listen to) ... and so to *ch 22 v 1,2* ... this is about the River of Life in the beautiful New Jerusalem which has come down from Heaven ... *v 7 and v 12* speak of the 'Catching Away of The Church' at the end of the Age of Grace ... the Lord Jesus is encouraging believers with these words 'Behold I am coming quickly' ...

My request to you, as the reader, is that you read *Revelation chapters 20, 21 and 22*, the last three chapters of the Bible, in one go - and take it slowly if you need to, in a good version of the Bible, to get more understanding and see the picture and the purposes of God's plan for you and everyone else. AMEN!

A Last PS!

I decided, in the writing of this book, not to go into 'Subjects' or 'Doctrine' which would make the substance of the book more complex than it is! .... so, when it came to problems of the world or things going wrong in Great Britain, I remained silent. As I write this, in December 2020, the Covid-19 Plague has given, and is still giving, directly or indirectly, many problems around the globe.

I'm addressing this especially to those who are asking, "What is this about? What does it all mean?" Well, we can't rule out the possibility of judgement from God for our sins, our wrongdoings .... but, repentance on a big scale, and putting wrongs right, would be big steps in the right direction! Some say, "Is this The Tribulation now?" .... the answer is, "No, it is **not**." It is like a small fraction of how The Tribulation will be, coming to us in the form of a plague, as a warning to Mankind that something e.g. Godlessness, is wrong, and God is not pleased and wants us to put it right. (Types of plagues can be horrific natural events etc.)

In my opinion, what is really happening currently is that what is going to be 'played out' in the actual Tribulation time has its background/whatever being put in place now as the scene is set in preparation for the **then** society being easily controlled, for evil, by the Antichrist, as Mankind is currently becoming accustomed to being controlled now. What the Antichrist will do to subdue Mankind on Earth will be possible through computer systems as he works to deceive people into believing that **he** is the real Messiah so that they will run after him, obey him and be caught up in his evil. This means that the void created by Godlessness and getting rid of Evangelical Christianity will be filled by the Antichrist. His control, coercive control, will be via his evil use of means scientific, social, medical, political and whatever, also by his harnessing of e.g. artificial intelligence, robotics and the media in his destruction of family units, and thus of society, and brainwashing of Mankind, as the enemies of God, into acceptance of the implanting of individual computer chips, some of which is already taking place ... and trying to refuse it will be no easy task. Even already, some of the medical stuff reported as happening now or getting underway e.g. interference with human genes, sounds terrible. Sadly too, Satanism (and every other kind of evil) is being openly pushed as if okay, normal and acceptable, while the Judeo-Christian truth of G.B. is being side-lined. Even the formerly, mostly respectable, Radio 4 now exalts Satanism and promotes the darker side of life, with its use of blasphemous language in some of its sexually immoral horror programmes etc. Evangelical Christianity, which made this nation great in the past, is sadly, at times, being ridiculed, with Evangelical Christian viewpoints being rare in news broadcasts. All this is here now in preparation for what is ahead in the 7- year Tribulation.

When doing Street Evangelism a few years back I used to ask myself, "What is it that has killed Christianity, as such, in this land?" ... then came to realise that the media and education have got the nation's mind and can generally turn it this way or that. I blamed 'Humanism' with the many things 'under its umbrella' (e.g. feminism, climate change) which, I believe, shows just like part of *Psalm 14 verse 1* states, 'The fool says in his heart, "There is no God" ....' Humanism can be summed up as Mankind saying, 'We have to sort out, by ourselves, everything that's wrong in the world'. In Humanism God is deliberately left out of the equation!!

Acknowledgements

Firstly, I give my loving thanks to Father God for enabling me to write this short book for His Glory .... I'm praying it will be a blessing to many! God is Love . . . . Glory!!

I'm very grateful to my dear, persevering (!) wife, Erika, for all her help and to all those who prayed for us both as I wrote, especially to our friends, Shirley and Eunike, who were closely involved from the start and gave such encouragement and faithful prayer support throughout. My wife and I wish to give our additional sincere thanks to Eunike for all her practical, willing help with I.T. and more!

Thank you all for your help towards the finished article!

I'm also very grateful to Amy Purdie, Whiteacres, for Cover Design etc.

Thank you Amy!

Henry, December 2020